Tell Me Why
WHY?
I See Rainbows

Kathryn Beaton

Published in the United States of America by Cherry Lake Publishing
Ann Arbor, Michigan

www.cherrylakepublishing.com

Content Adviser: Jack Williams, science writer specializing in weather
Reading Adviser: Marla Conn, ReadAbility, Inc.

Photo Credits: © Pete Pahham/Shutterstock Images, cover, 1, 5; © Dalton Dingelstad/Shutterstock
Images, cover, 1, 19; © Digital Media Pro/Shutterstock Images, cover, 1, 13; © Capricornis Photographic
Inc./Shutterstock Images, cover, 15; © voylodyon/Shutterstock Images, cover; © Nneirda/Shutterstock
Images, cover, 9; © Patryk Kosmider/Shutterstock Images, 5; © Belkos/Shutterstock Images, 7;
© wattana/Shutterstock Images, 11; © 360b/Shutterstock Images, 13; © racorn/Shutterstock Images, 17;
© Pierre Leclerc/Shutterstock Images, 19; © bjonesphotography/Shutterstock Images, 21

Library of Congress Cataloging-in-Publication Data

Beaton, Kathryn.
 I see rainbows / by Kathryn Beaton.
    pages cm -- (Tell me why)
 Includes index.
 Summary: "Young children are naturally curious about the world around
them. I See Rainbows offers answers to their most compelling questions about
rainbows. Age-appropriate explanations and appealing photos encourage
readers to continue their quest for knowledge. Additional text features and
search tools, including a glossary and an index, help students locate
information and learn new words"—Provided by publisher.
 Audience: 6-10.
 Audience: K-Grade 3.
 ISBN 978-1-63188-997-4 (hardcover) -- ISBN 978-1-63362-075-9 (pdf) -- ISBN
978-1-63362-036-0 (pbk.) -- ISBN 978-1-63362-114-5 (ebook)
 1. Rainbows--Juvenile literature. I. Title. II. Series: Tell me why (Cherry Lake Publishing)

 QC976.R2B43 2015
 551.56'7--dc23

                    2014031837

Cherry Lake Publishing would like to acknowledge the work of The Partnership for 21st Century Skills.
Please visit www.21.org for more information.

Printed in the United States of America
Corporate Graphics

Table of Contents

A Rainbow at Recess

No recess for Caitlin and her classmates this afternoon. They all stayed indoors because it was raining. Caitlin pulled out a piece of paper and her markers and began to draw. She was surprised when a **ray** of sunlight passed over her paper. She looked out the window and saw something else surprising. A rainbow!

"Look!" she called.

Do you think rainbows appear more often in the summer or the winter? Go online with an adult or visit your library to get the answer.

Rainbows happen only during rainy weather.

Everyone went to the window and looked outside. A giant **arc** striped with lots of colors was shining above the soccer field.

"Wow," Caitlin said. "How does that happen?"

Her teacher, Miss Burton, smiled. "Since the storm is over, let's go outside. I'll tell you about rainbows in science class later."

Caitlin kept wondering about the rainbow. She could still see it in the sky.

Rainbows appear when it is rainy and sunny at the same time.

The Right Conditions

After recess Caitlin asked Miss Burton where rainbows come from.

"Rainbows need two things," her teacher said. "Sunshine and water. And both have to be there at the same time."

"That doesn't happen much," said Max, one of Caitlin's friends.

"That's right," Miss Burton said. "It sometimes happens near the end of a storm. First, the light from the sun shines through the rainwater. Then the rain **reflects** all the colors back at us."

Rainbows sometimes appear in a waterfall or near its spray if the sun is shining.

"Let's talk a little about how sunlight works," Miss Burton said. She explained that the rays from the sun are different sizes. Light with a long **wavelength** looks red to us. Light with a short wavelength looks violet. The medium-sized wavelengths make **shades** of orange, yellow, and green.

"So the sunlight can be different colors?" Caitlin asked.

"Not exactly," Miss Burton said. "We just *see* different colors."

short

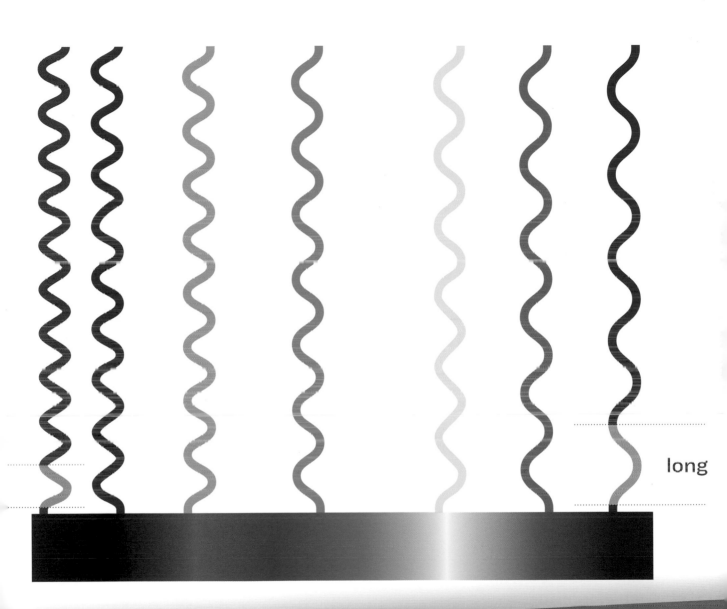

long

Violet has the shortest wavelength. Red has the longest wavelength.

White Light and Raindrops

A ray of sunlight is white light. White light is made up of all the colors combined. When this white light hits the rain, all the rays change directions. Each color we see depends on the **angle** of the sunlight reflecting off each raindrop. The white light's angle changes as it passes through the raindrops. This makes the raindrops reflect all the colors.

"Okay," Max said. "But where was the rain?"

"Yeah," Caitlin said. "It was sunny on the playground."

Are there any colors that you don't see in this rainbow?

When the sun's white light passes through rain drops,
colors are reflected.

"Right," Miss Burton said. "The sun was behind us. For a rainbow to appear, it has to be sunny where you're standing but raining in the distance."

"So it was raining on the soccer field?" Caitlin asked.

"Farther away than that," Miss Burton said. "The rain clouds must have moved across town. But if the weather is exactly right, rainbows can happen anywhere in the world."

We see this rainbow because it is raining on the other side of the buildings, and the sun is behind the photographer.

A Trick of the Light

Max was using crayons to draw a rainbow. His rainbow looked different from the one outside. "I only used my favorite colors," he said.

"That's very creative, Max," Miss Burton said. Then she told the class that the colors in a natural rainbow always appear in the same order.

Drawing a rainbow with markers and crayons helps you remember the colors of a natural rainbow.

She wrote "ROY G. BIV" on the whiteboard. "This is an easy way to remember the order of the colors. It stands for red, orange, yellow, green, blue, **indigo**, and violet. You can't always see them all, but red is always on top, and violet is always on the bottom."

"I have another question," Caitlin said. "What's at the ends of a rainbow? What holds it up?"

MAKE A GUESS!

The colors in these two rainbows appear in the opposite order. Can you guess why this would happen?

The first and brighter rainbow is called a primary rainbow. The second and more faint rainbow is called a secondary rainbow.

"A rainbow isn't solid," Miss Burton said. "It's just a trick of the light. If you walked close enough to touch it, it would just disappear."

"Look!" said Max. He pointed to the window, and the class crowded around. "The rainbow is gone!"

Miss Burton smiled. "They don't stay for very long," she said. "That's what makes them so special."

You can make your own rainbow by spraying a garden hose on a sunny day when the sun is directly behind your head.

Think About It

You can create your own rainbow! Ask your parents for help using a garden hose. Hold it up to the sunlight and put your thumb over the end when it sprays. Do you see a little rainbow across your garden? Try twisting the nozzle to adjust the size of the water droplets. What happens?

Find something in your house that's small and that you have many colors of. Think of beads, building blocks, crayons, or fruit-flavored cereal. See if you can arrange the objects into arcs on a table, using ROY G. BIV to help. Take a photo!

Glossary

angle (ANG-guhl) the figure formed by two lines extending from the same point

arc (ARK) a line shaped like a half circle

indigo (IN-di-goh) dark bluish-purple

ray (RAY) a narrow beam of light coming from the sun

reflects (ri-FLEKTS) bounces off an object

shades (SHAYDZ) degrees of darkness in colors

wavelength (WAYV-lengkth) the distance between two high points in a wave

Find Out More

Books:

Cole, Joanna. *The Magic School Bus Makes a Rainbow*. New York City: Scholastic Inc., 1997.

Rajczak, Kristen. *Nature's Light Show: Rainbows*. New York City: Gareth Stevens Publishing, 2013.

Snedeker, Joe. *The Everything Kids' Weather Book*. Avon, MA: Adams Media, 2012.

Web Sites:

HowStuffWorks: How Rainbows Work
http://science.howstuffworks.com/nature/climate-weather/storms/rainbow.htm
Learn about how the right combination of rain and sunlight can form this beautiful phenomenon.

The Imagination Tree: 40 Fantastic Rainbow Activities for Kids!
http://theimaginationtree.com/2013/02/40-fantastic-rainbow-activities-for-kids.html
Learn how to make tons of different rainbow-related crafts—jewelry, cookies, wall art, and more.

National Geographic: Patterns in Nature: Rainbows
http://photography.nationalgeographic.com/photography/photos/patterns-nature-rainbows/
Check out this amazing slide show of rainbows from all over the world.

Index

About the Author

Kathryn Beaton lives and writes in Ann Arbor, Michigan.